I0393443

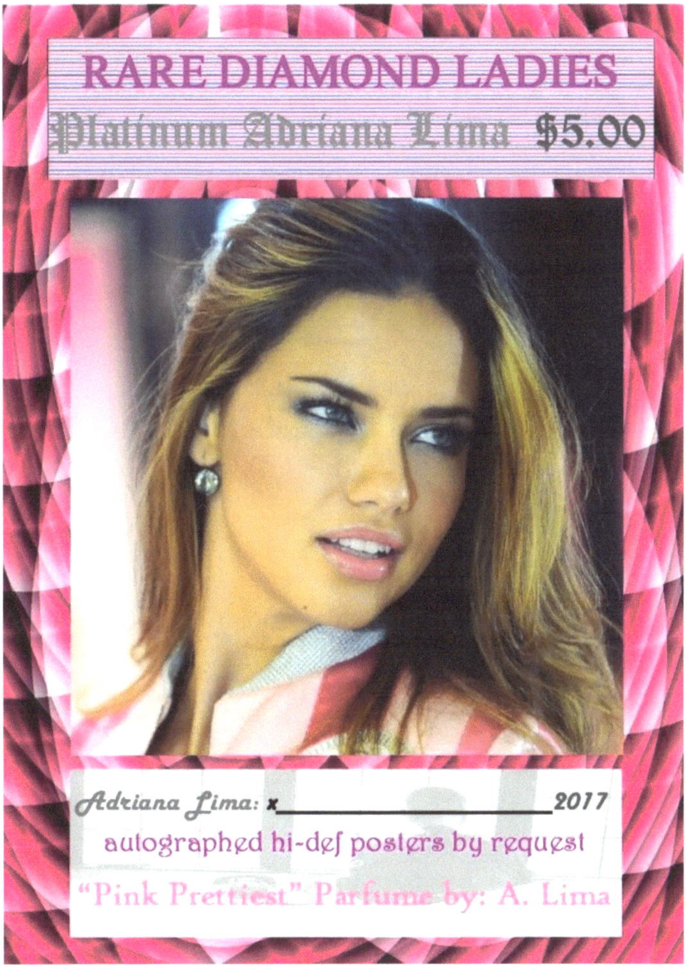

RARE DIAMOND LADIES
Platinum Adriana Lima $5.00

Adriana Lima: **x**_____*2017*

autographed hi-def posters by request

"Pink Prettiest" Parfume by: A. Lima

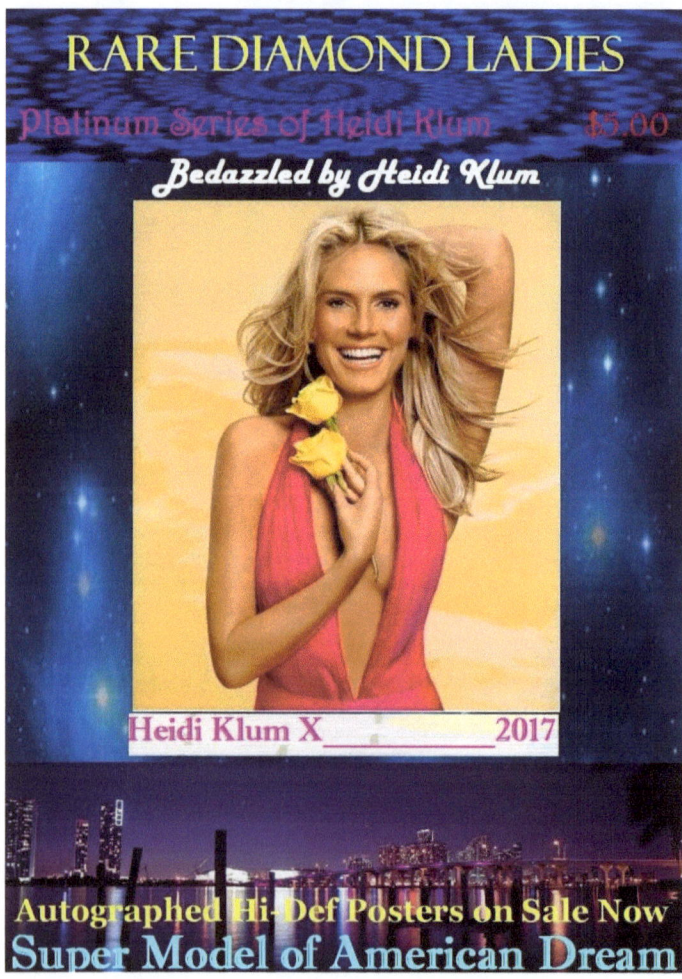

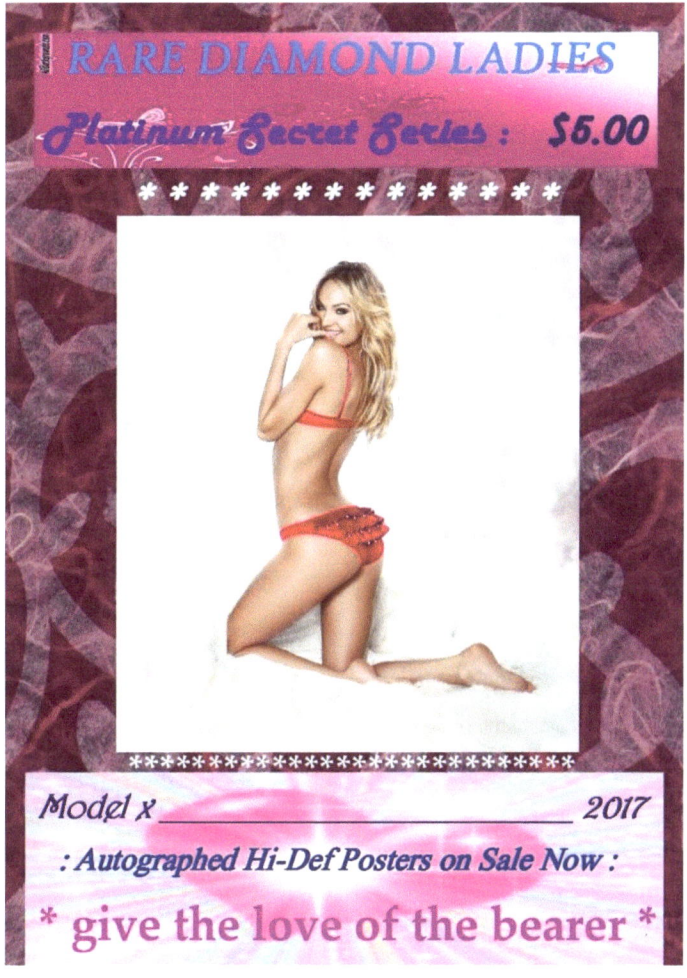

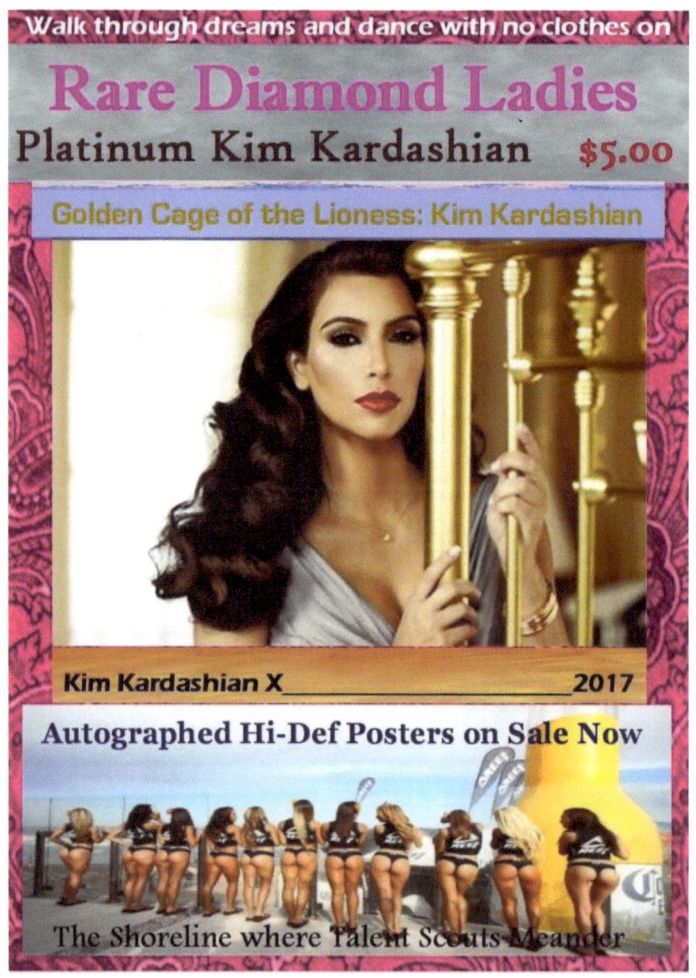

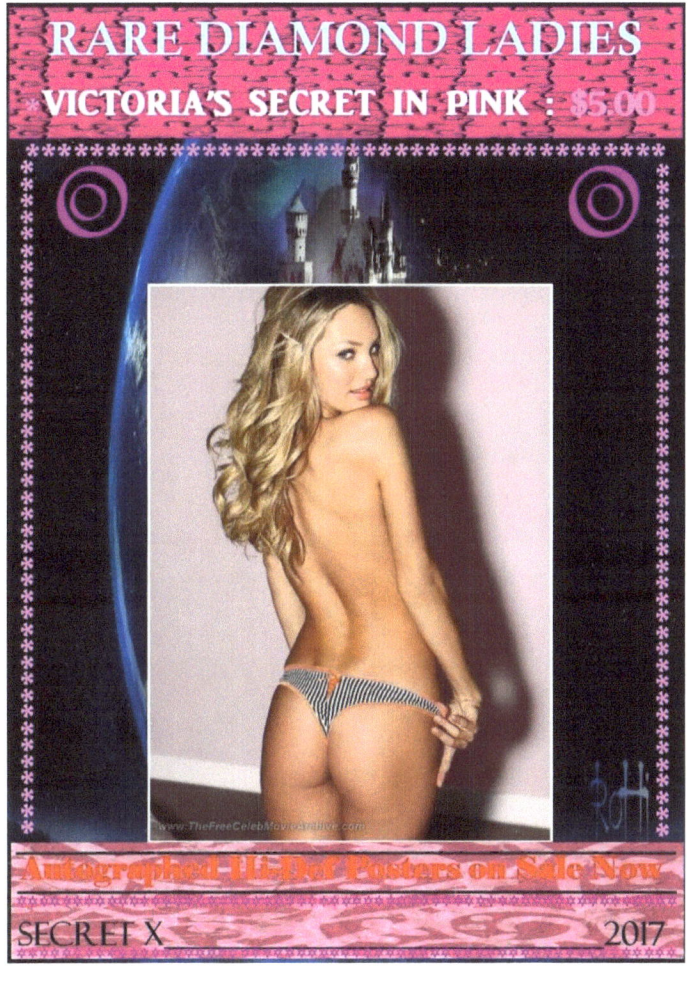

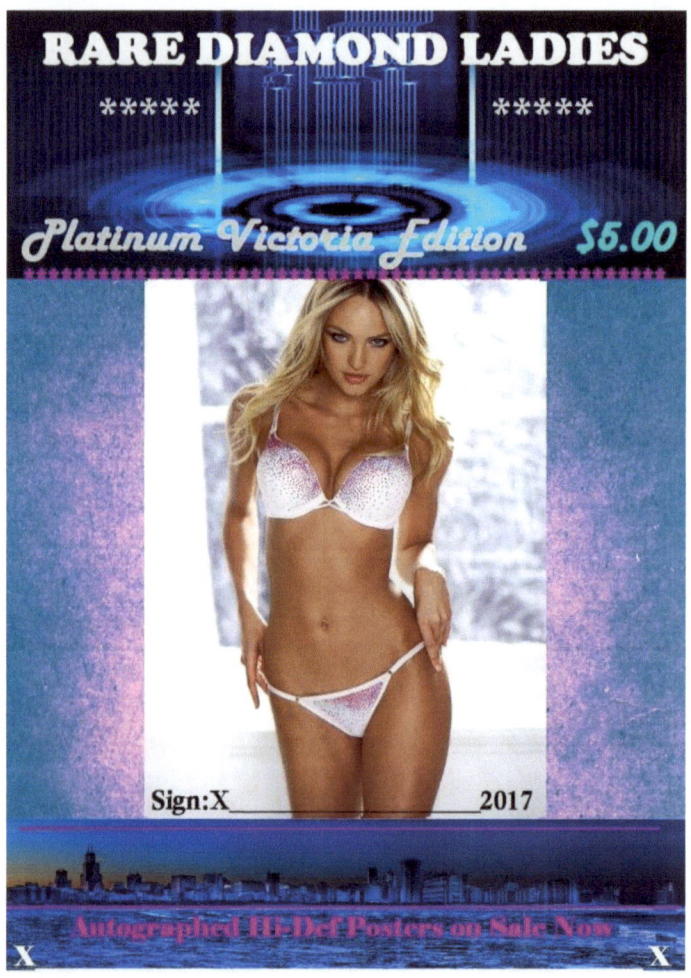

RARE DIAMOND LADIES

Platinum : Shakira : $5.00

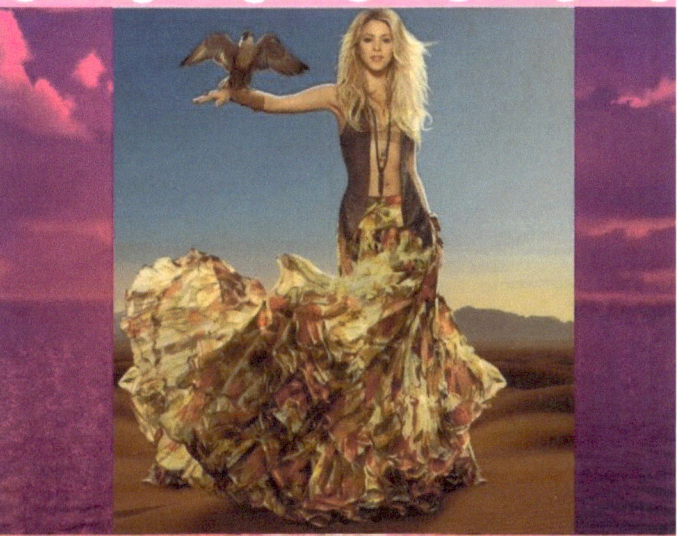

Shakira x_____ *2017*

Autographed H-Def Posters on Sale Now

All She Wants To Be : Shakira

Record of The Bird Flight

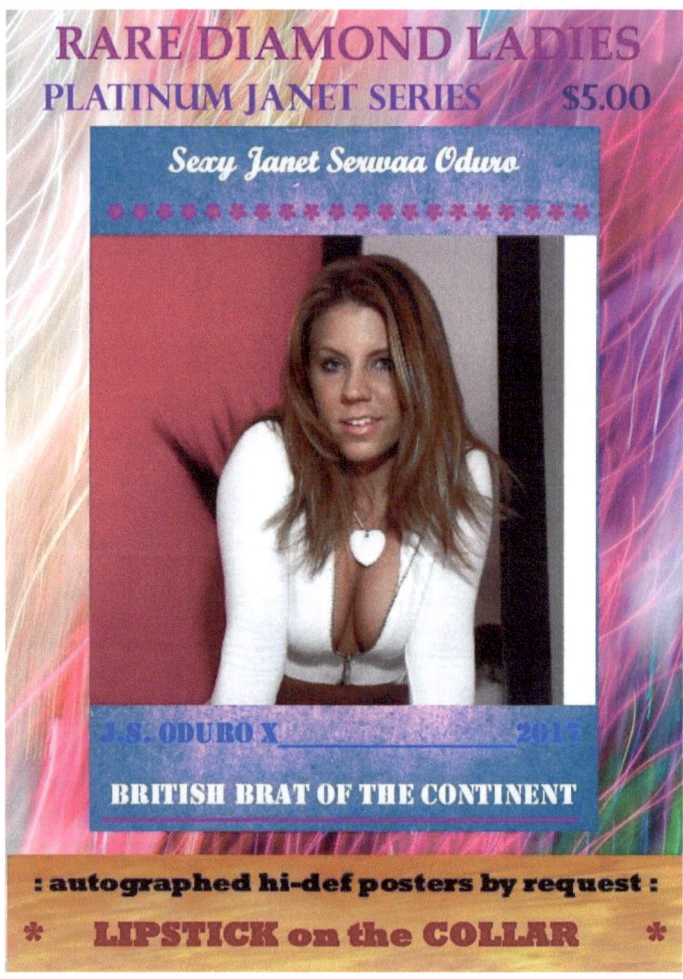

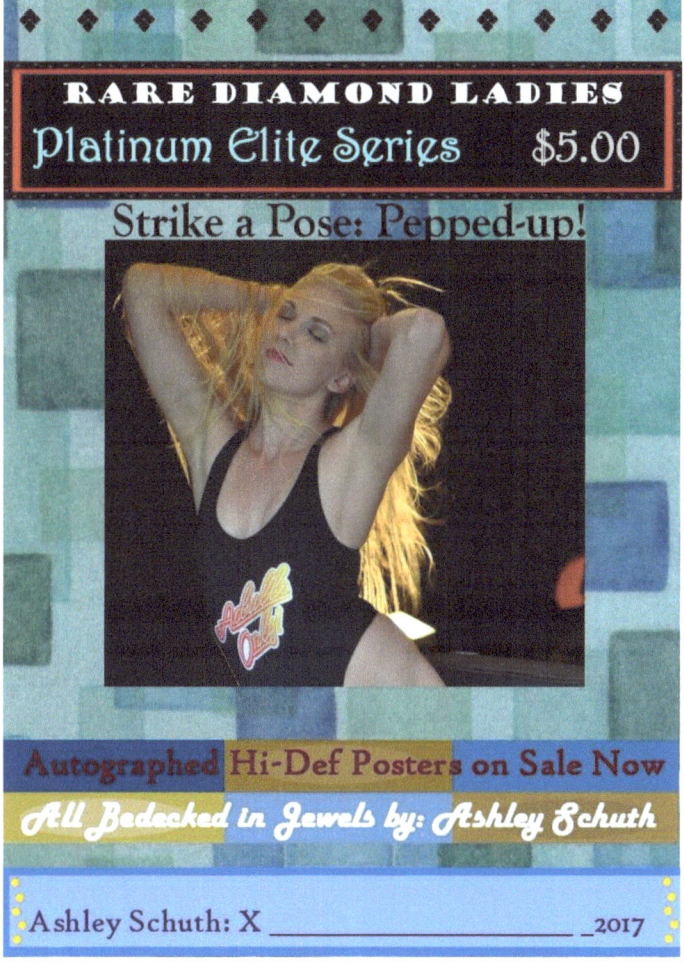

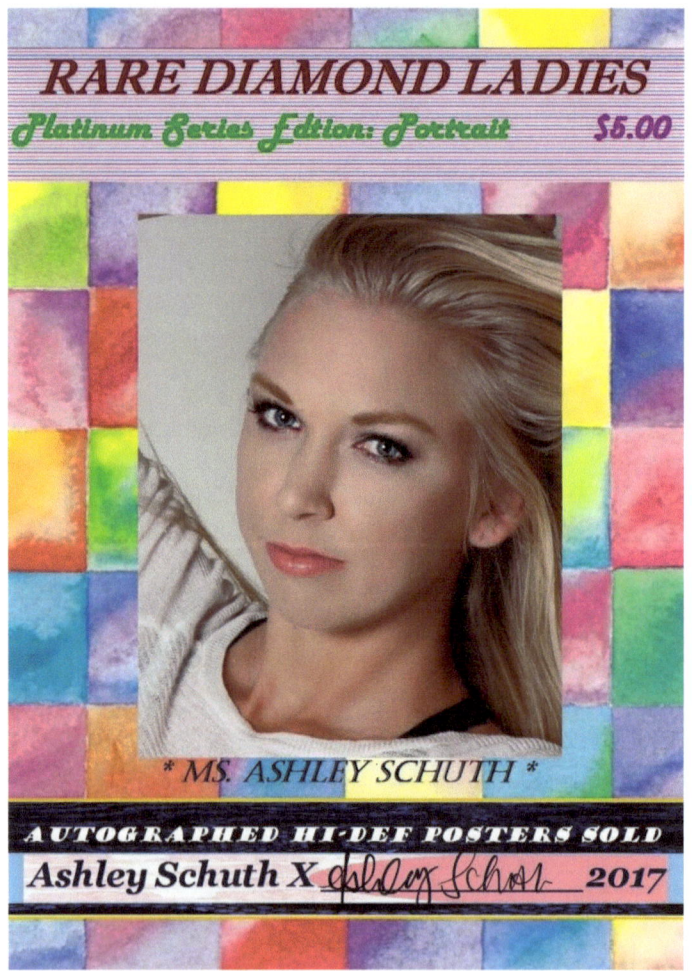

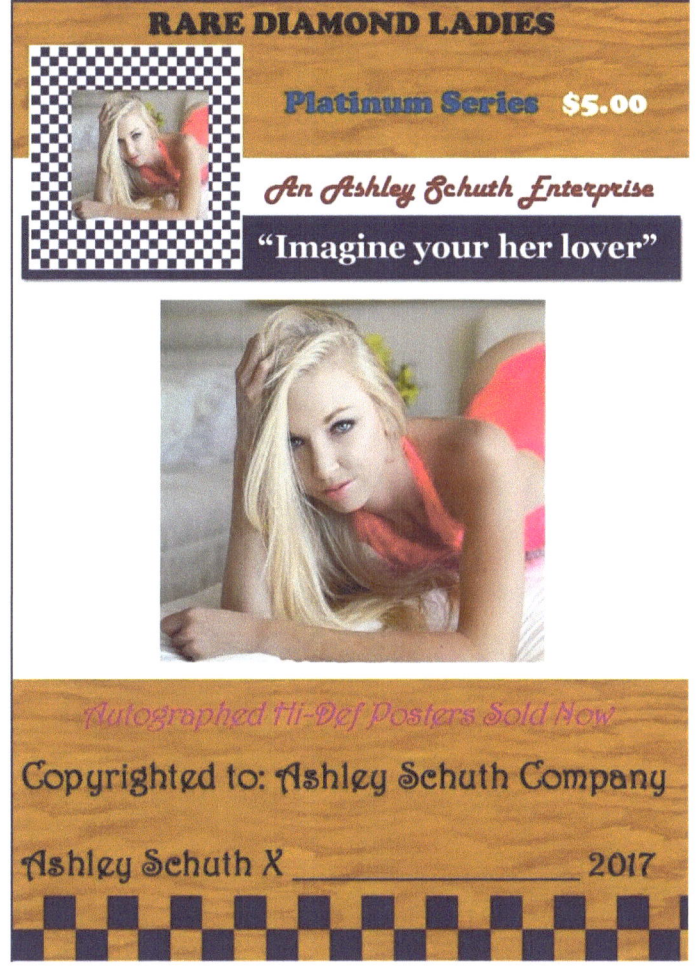

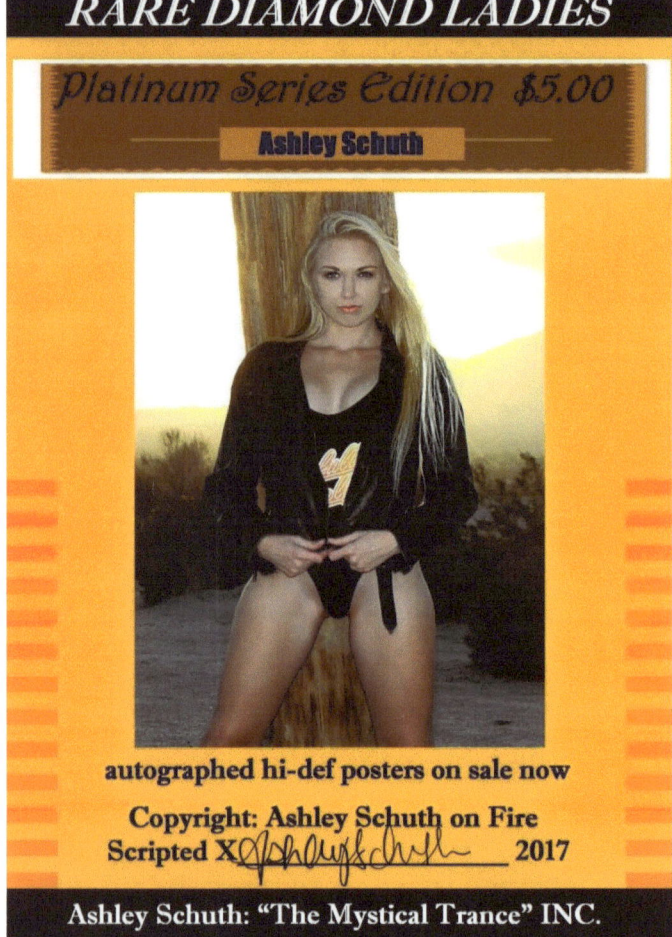

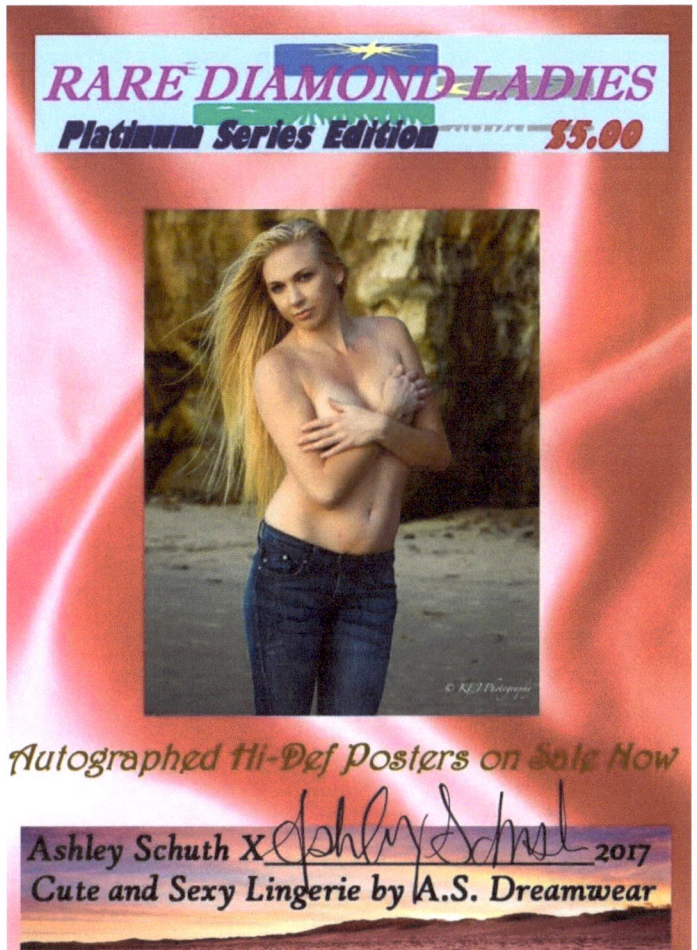

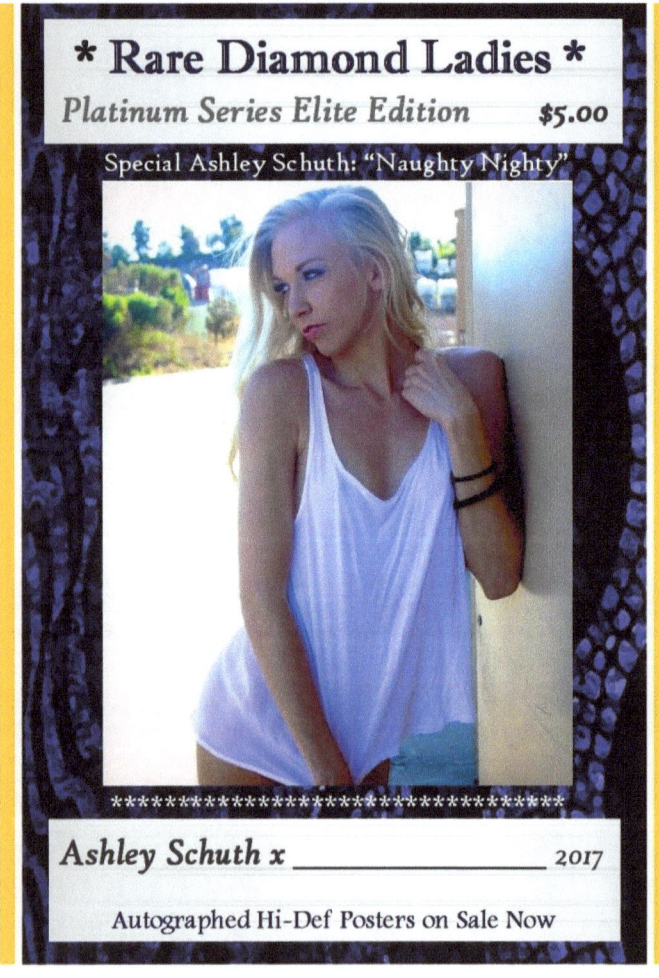

Rare Diamond Ladies

Platinum Series Edition $5.00

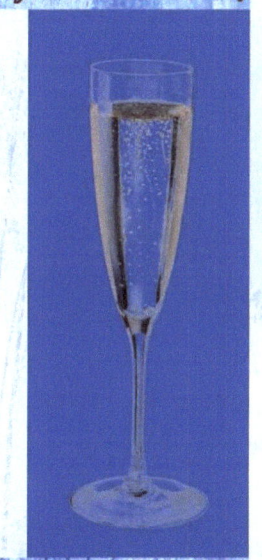
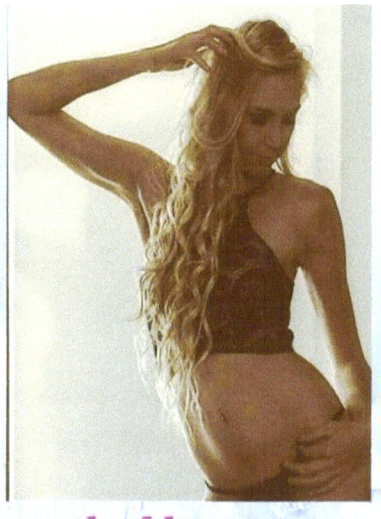

touched by treasure

autographed hi-def poster sales

Ashley Schuth: Goddess of Wine

Ashley Schuth X _____ 2017

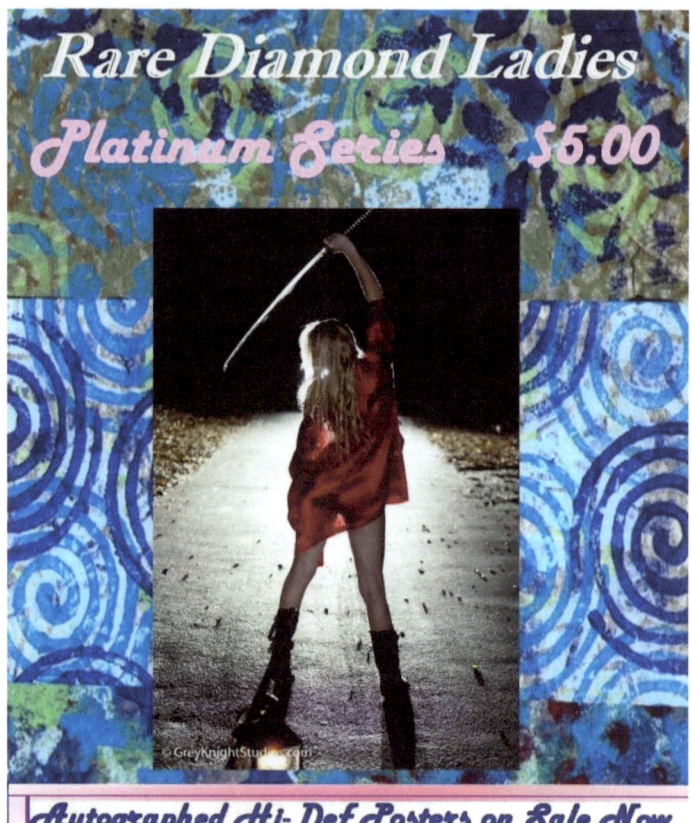

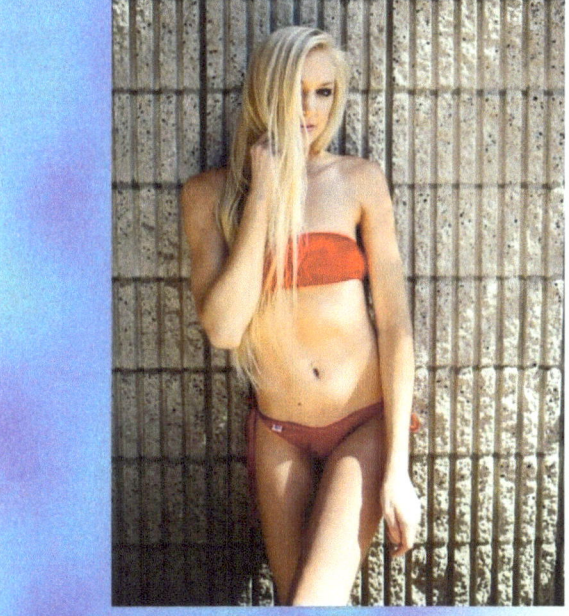

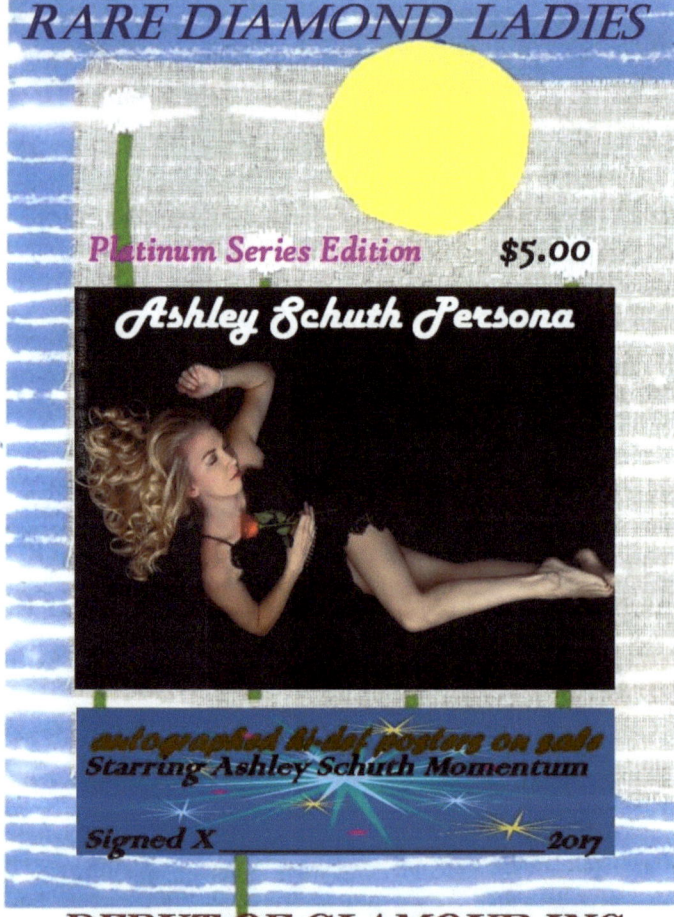

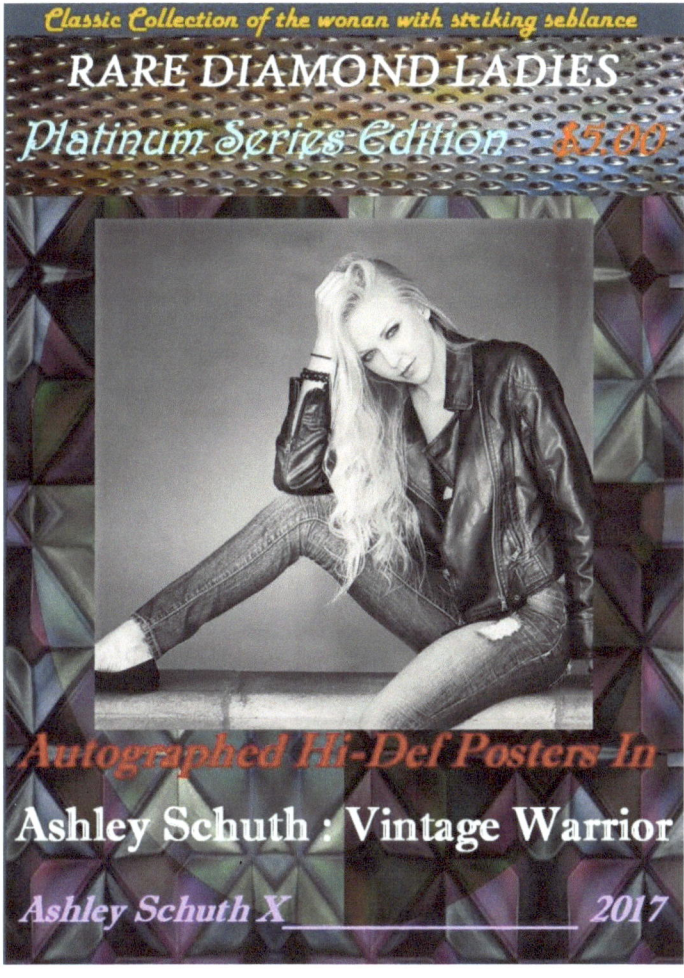

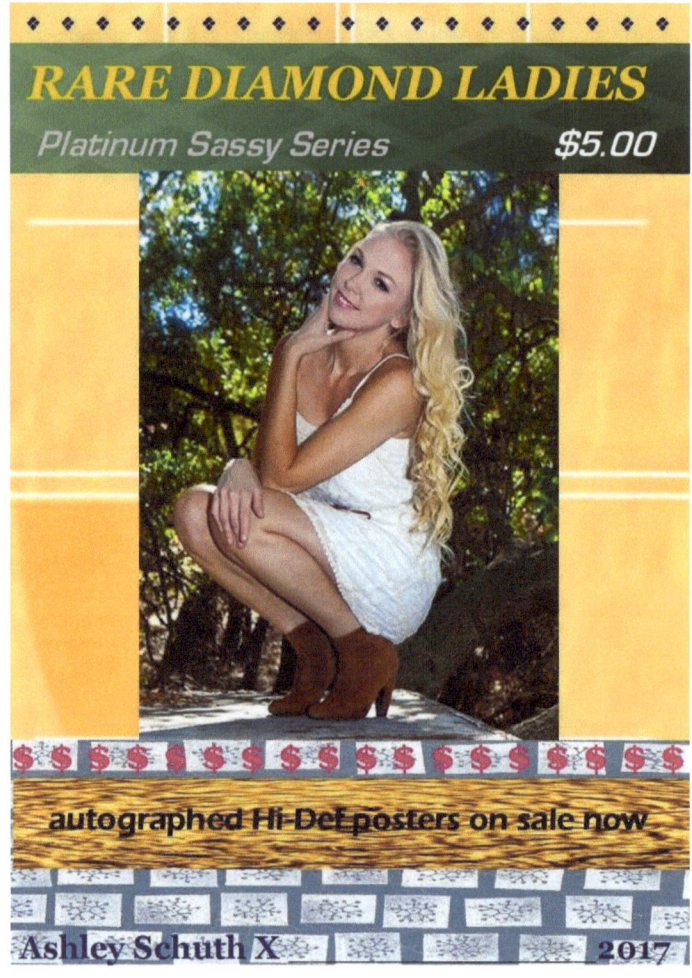

Dear Hillary:

I don't believe in masculine equal pay for a woman. That is the Flintstone monetary code of Adam. Do you comprehend this? To further explain it to you, men bartered deer antlers for cash or flints or beer or tobacco, and such the like. The female monetary code in your labors as nurturers of at least childbirth are a different set of values vs bearded dominators. These start with a feminine think tank process and to extrapolate your true yearnings for the goddess of love... meaning a child is priceless to man, whether male or female; the DNA is still intact. Though man is not meant to pay for your labor. You decide your needs and place a code to them, as often found in diamonds and silk, if this is a royal concordance of feminine equity. You are still the lioness... the highest archetype of woman. If the lioness does not submit herself to the lion, the lion will not abjectly submit his seed to Elsa. Ending rape through exploitation by pornography. You could sue man for this gross parade of adultery, and save youth from fornication, another potential lawsuit of male cub killers. Example A. College Co-Eds and Cheerleaders, that were 18 years of age (legal?) and wanton youth must be over age 21 to view the expose'. Although now internet touts an age 18 range for both sexes, but only for the income of vulgarity. You see it's income, and not intimacy. The love of money is the root of all evil. Noted as lust and greed. Do not look at the perverted femininity of men-said. Look at the riches that are lasting for the love nest, not in intercourse. But in union with the goddess tribe of a value that deserves the exceeding bounty, above man. Be not weighed down with bobbles or script, that is demonic. Create a system that gives easy access to the survival (essential needs) of mankind, by and for woman.

David Pedjoe
http://www.zhibit.org/artlink,

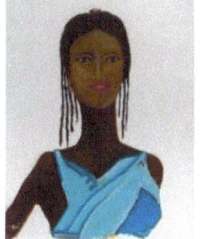

Date: Thu, 28 Apr 2016 21:18:18 +0000
From: info@hillaryclinton.com
To: davidpedjoe@outlook.com
Subject: A Woman Card just for you

☆ International Copyright & Patent: Ashley Schuth ☆

Lovely Ashley of the Morning Dawn:

I cometh to bring you prizes from a mad scientist with a heart of gold. Be very careful to keep in trust all the love I give, you got. Here is a beauty treatment from my labs. Keep it secret; then patent it and you'll be "Sweetly Pinkend" with the surprise I have wrought. Sorry I peeked at your prettie that dulled light tan. But I have a new creation, and don't be scared. We begin the process with the prettie shaved, then wipe off the cream and feel so new. Now comes the wizard of dreams. Be not fearful, all will work out. But I did the experiment on my pink one myself. Tested true to all who dare, the treatment is: we start with this: Crest 3D White: Radiant Mint. Apply about a level tablespoon of toothpaste to all your major labia, rub in and let dry all morning, not to remove residue. In afternoon check your area and it should be redden with flakes of white. Attempt to wipe off in fear? Do not fear!!! Use water only. You'll get frightened. Let dry. When evening tide comes, and you still look diseased? Apply CVS pharmacy: firming moisturizer Q10 (order online if not available in your locale) Co-enzyme Q10 complex. Rub in application our your surface area. Dry a little bit with air. Wipe off with white wet facecloth and you will be baby pink. Tested by inventor personally: David M Pedjoe. Now powder with Gold Bond Powder and enjoy the rare beauty of being young again. If there is further issues with light tan. Use Strong Cream on area:

Copyright Patent to: Ashley Schuth X_____12/16/2016

DAVID M PEDJOE

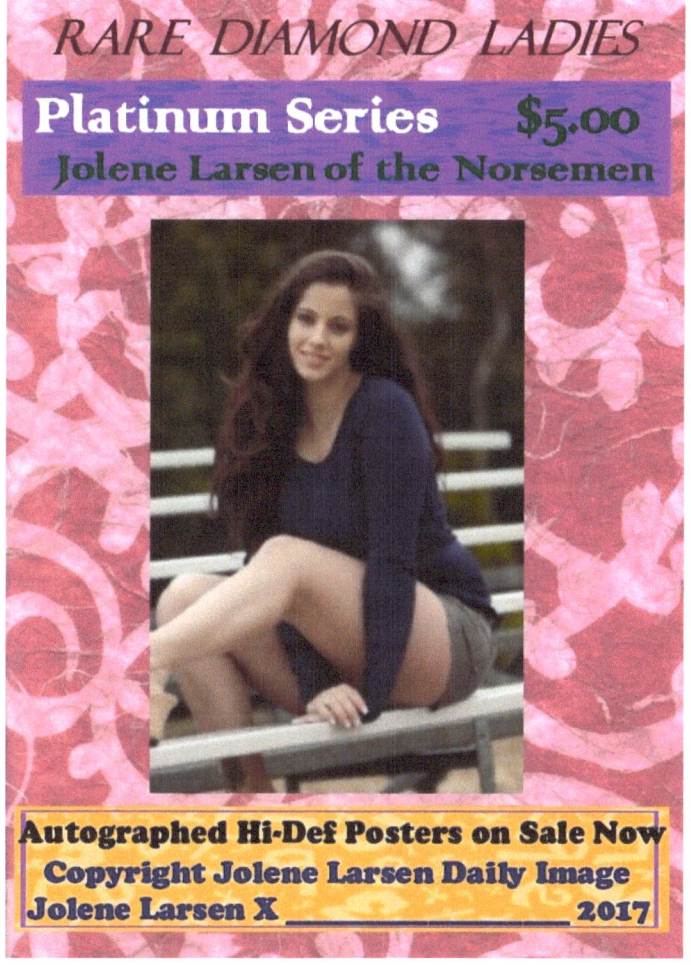

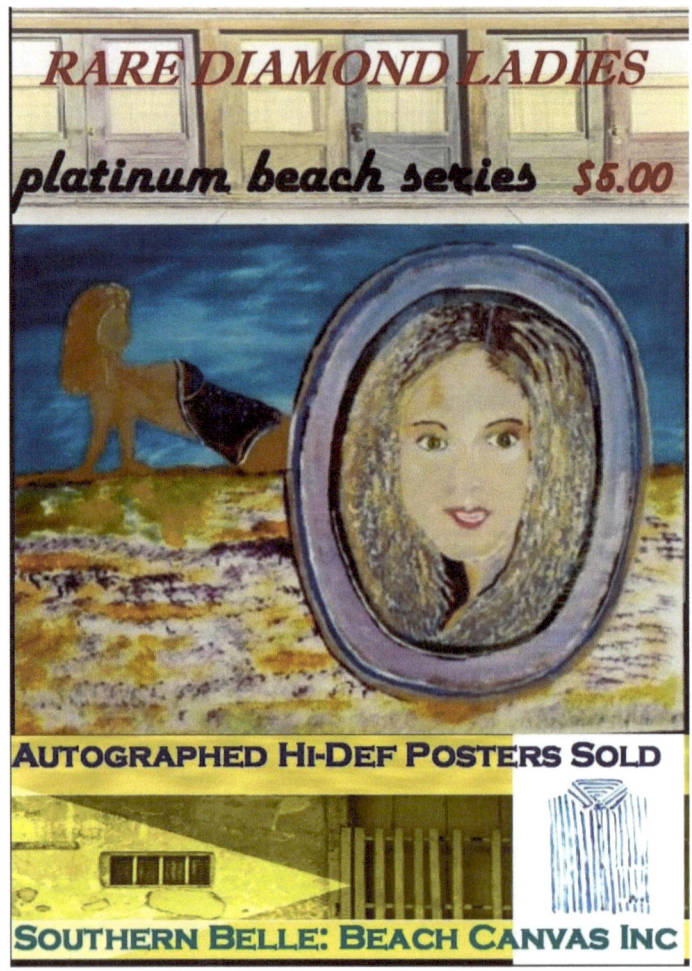

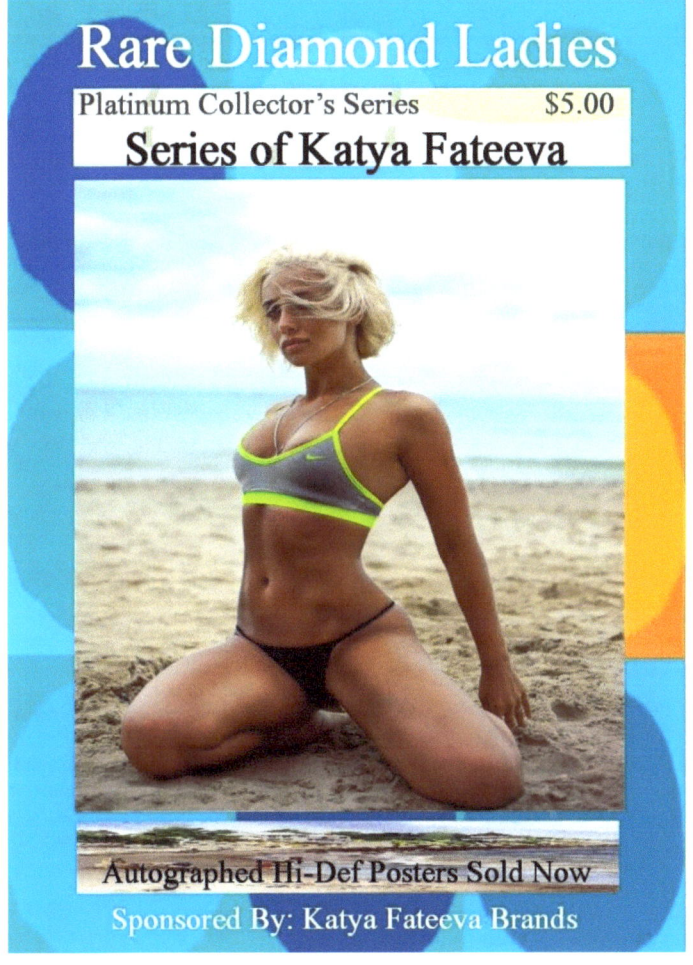

Envision yourself on my portico, as we indulge with ice tea and caviar with toast triangles and farmers chess. It is a warm and breezy starlit night. You look dazzling in your refined attire, an artist's dream? I smile upon you and gaze to hearts content, with no lust in mine being. Such is the beauty of youth, the becoming sensation of my portraiture. I place in your hand a sparkling diamond as a token of appreciation. The night lingers on with laughter and patiently we prepare each and other for the studio, where I will paint you.

The time has come, we retreat into my living quarters, not holding hands or making goo-goo eyes upon you. This is professional business ethics, with none but the Masters brushes to capture you on canvas. You prepare to pose in elegant lingerie, my stamina increases to do a perfect masterpiece. You are on a tufted bed of navy blue velour and golden pillows. You relax and our company is no longer, that of a stranger. The room is scented by your perfume, your bath robe hangs on the bed post. I see you clearly now and we whisper as the brushstrokes wet the gesso on the canvas panel. You yawn and grow weary... I say: do not be afraid, there is none crime, when I am a knight and protector. You dose off, as I concentrate mine Merlin magic. The night will fulfill your dreams as I create the mightiness of your image, through the deed I am gifted with. Paint is mixed and colors flow, I do not intend to copy your attire and improvise with mine own designer wear. I see the impression, then again I challenge myself to fine art with acrylics. The sky begins to lighten and it is finished.

You awaken with no disturbances and I say good morning. Surprising you with sparkling champagne with a rose in the flute. Voila, I claim and show you the portrait. It is yours to keep with copyrights included. You moan and smile with awe. Compliment me as a gentleman. Hoping we could celebrate this way once again. I bow slightly and proclaim: "It would be my pleasure, young lady." A drug and alcohol-free meeting of creation. A perfect lady and a perfect gentleman. Who would disagree? Why? Jealousy: which is a sin to man. Beware of saboteurs. The diamond sparkles!

Wrought of you by:
David Pedjoe

CONFIDENTIALITY

PERSONAL INFORMATION (please print or type)

Your Name: David Michael Pedjoe

Idea Name: "The Stealth"

Street Address: 21 Cypress Avenue City: Shrewsbury State/Prov: MA Zip/Postal Code: 01545-1368

Telephone: Residence (best) 845-0642 Business ( ) Same When is the best time to call? 24/7

BACKGROUND INFORMATION

My idea for a New Product is...

"The Stealth" Sanitary Napkin.
Absorbent Pad, Contralized
Quilted by "feather" design
Contoured, with "fin" to hold
in place.
Creates "Stealth" Sanitized"

I came up with my idea when I was...

Studying Toxic Shock Syndrome
Back When People Were Dying?

(Roughly Sketch your idea in this space)

Insert

Inner Absorbency   Quilted Lips

AGREEMENT

I believe, to the best of my knowledge, that I am the original inventor of the idea described herein. I hereby authorize Davison to provide me a no-cost discussion about my idea, with no purchase required. I understand submitting my concept is not a release and that this information cannot be used, disclosed, or sold without my expressed written permission. I also understand that all employees of Davison are required to sign an ethics and confidentiality agreement for my protection. By signing this agreement I understand that Davison does not promise or guarantee any financial gain from the development of any new product or idea.

David M. Pedjoe 11/3/04   John M. Lojoe 11/3/04 DAP
Client   Date   Client   Date

Acknowledged by: M. Davison   (Authorized Davison signature)

PLEASE FAX TOLL FREE OR RETURN WHITE COPY IN THE POSTAGE PAID ENVELOPE

Davison, Inc., RIDC Park, 595 Alpha Drive, Pittsburgh, PA 15238-2911   Phone: 1-800-56 ideas   Fax Toll Free: 1-800-540-5490
www.1800s4ideas.com

Dear Super Models:
I have interest once again to reiterate your plans to hold out on nudity, for as long as you can, but certainly before your wallowing in the mire. Being put out to pasture, was a warning my (passed-on) Mom... taught me about to save you girls from rainy-days. My Dad and John Robert Powers Modeling Agency had nothing to do with me as an artisan / photographer. Well there were assets donated to me, by Dad... and once he said your family is with you in spirit. I noted Jacqueline Bouvier was once a JRP girl and models were paid $2,000.00 a shoot. I also offered scholarships to JRP on mine own... so Dad wouldn't go to hell. The payment agreement I read and knew about some twice 90 day deal, that added up to six months before granted payment. But Mom was also a model of wigs and an off-Broadway actress, had me in youth... try out for: "South Pacific" and Ms. Clifford had me as the King in "The Tax King" Play. As I was dressed up a English Lord in a long red jacket and ruffled black shorts and black tights: "I am your King" and vowed to pay you back! This is just a synapsis of my life that led to esteem your progress as I calculated the persona you could attain. It began with "Pink" and the backstage "meet and greet" for $75,000.00 dollars, when the greats only got $20,000.00 for a three day layover in on average NY. NY. and Los Angelus. That dude wasn't driving modeling careers to obsolete annihilation. Therefore I intervened. First with Paula Jones and a $ Million USD kiss. Then I calculated the real results of... what I say again? Well actually it's more than just nudity... it's a three hundred photograph shoot = I can handle 800 photos on my 4 GB San Disk and take the shoot in one day via Jet Blue to Worcester MA. 01602 USA. I will arrange airfare and Hong Kong attire and I'll keep a copy of the photos, only allowing me to create photo story 3 videos with, that I email to you anyways. But you keep the clothes, the camera and the San Disk... then we would allocate the photos into high-definition prints @ $ 3000.00 USD per print, created by publisher and earning income of prints x 800 I would hope. Then being famous (without nudity) you would earn through saturation marketing, as onto Picasso or the price of $ 100,000.00 USD per personally autographed pictures, in an unlimited series, as unto the Farrah Fawcett "pink" bath-suit. That mistakenly had a stamped on signature... that ruined her famed value. Now you know. This should not happen to you. You have evolved as a model, and in demand... as wolves hunger for your, in the buff; composure... still not attained and need it not. The tease, creates a challenge and your haunted by chump-change porn images that disgust you. But if you did, the likes of Esquire your nudity would fetch $ One Billion Dollars! How? Do you know how many magazines would sell? You did the David and Jesus trick? The advertisers would pay big bucks for image in the pages of High-end Markets. You get the copyrights to the image and sell ads and rake in $ One Billion USD for just a few of the business hook-biters. Never mind the magazine itself, and the fact you sold all thee advertisements. Models comprehend this as well as you gentlemen of agreement. Congratulations... your now valued in assets near Two Billion USD. Here's an easy $ 2 Billion for Vanessa Williams = a rebel of tradition. Instant Fame! Instant Gratuities! Fiat!
David M Pedjoe

www.ingramcontent.com/pod-product-compliance
Lightning Source LLC
Chambersburg PA
CBHW041133200526
45172CB00018B/350